For Max—
a kid who truly rocks—K. S.

For Aliza,
you ROCK star!—S. S.

BEACH LANE BOOKS
An imprint of Simon & Schuster Children's Publishing Division
1230 Avenue of the Americas, New York, New York 10020
Text © 2025 by Katie Slivensky
Illustration © 2025 by Steph Stilwell
Book design by Steph Stilwell and Lauren Rille
All rights reserved, including the right of reproduction in whole or in part in any form.
BEACH LANE BOOKS and colophon are trademarks of Simon & Schuster, LLC.
For information about special discounts for bulk purchases, please contact Simon & Schuster Special Sales
at 1-866-506-1949 or business@simonandschuster.com.
The Simon & Schuster Speakers Bureau can bring authors to your live event.
For more information or to book an event, contact the Simon & Schuster Speakers Bureau
at 1-866-248-3049 or visit our website at www.simonspeakers.com.
The text for this book was set in Londrina.
The illustrations for this book were hand drawn, then colored digitally in Adobe Photoshop.
Manufactured in China
0225 SCP • First Edition
10 9 8 7 6 5 4 3 2 1
Library of Congress Cataloging-in-Publication Data • Names: Slivensky, Katie, author. | Stilwell, Steph, illustrator. • Title: I, rock : a geology tale / Katie Slivensky, Steph Stilwell. • Description: New York : Beach Lane Books, 2025. | Includes bibliographical references. | Audience: Ages 4–8 | Audience: Grades 2–3 | Summary: "Rock tells his sensational, sometimes harrowing, sometimes hilarious, geological tale to a group of eager students"— Provided by publisher. • Identifiers: LCCN 2024033516 (print) | LCCN 2024033517 (ebook) | ISBN 9781665940368 (hardcover) | ISBN 9781665940375 (ebook) • Subjects: LCSH: Rocks—Juvenile literature. • Classification: LCC QE432.2 .S635 2025 (print) | LCC QE432.2 (ebook) | DDC 552—dc23 /eng20241010 • LC record available at https://lccn.loc.gov/2024033516 • LC ebook record available at https://lccn.loc.gov/2024033517

I ROCK

A Geology Tale

words by
KATIE SLIVENSKY

pictures by
STEPH STILWELL

Beach Lane Books
New York Amsterdam/Antwerp London Toronto Sydney New Delhi

Ah! There we go. I couldn't help but hear your class sharing stories about the oldest people you know.

I noticed none of those stories are from folks who have been around quite as long as me, though. Would anyone like to hear a four-billion-year-old's story? I might not look like much, but—

I started out in the deep, dark underground.
Not quite liquid, not quite solid, not quite me.
That's where I got to know my minerals.

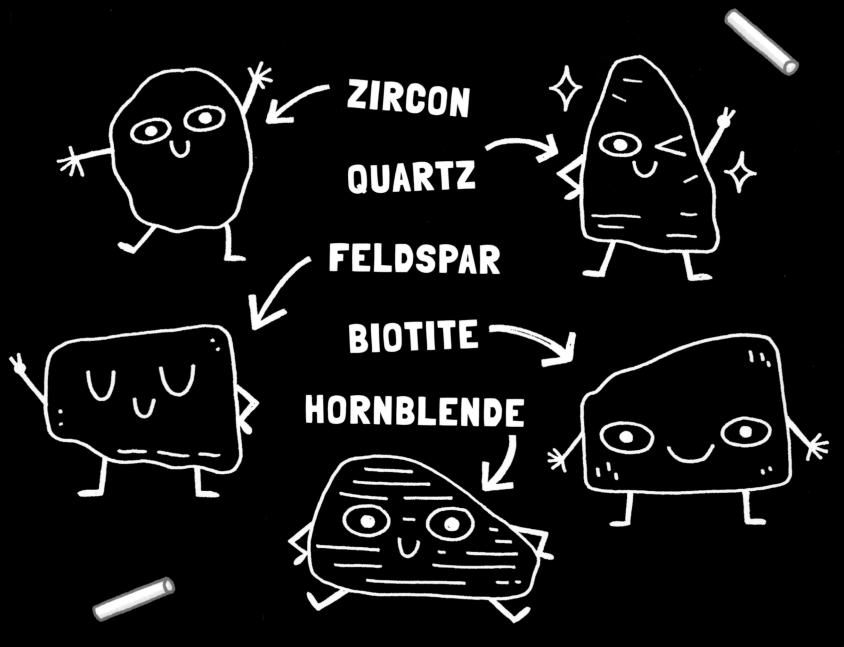

ZIRCON

QUARTZ

FELDSPAR

BIOTITE

HORNBLENDE

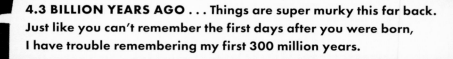

4.3 BILLION YEARS AGO . . . Things are super murky this far back.
Just like you can't remember the first days after you were born,
I have trouble remembering my first 300 million years.

What are minerals? They're the ingredients that make rocks! They can make us . . .

SUPER STRONG.

SHARP. SPARKLY!

And, my personal favorite, **able to withstand BURNING ACID.**

4 BILLION YEARS AGO . . .
Introducing . . . my minerals! They really get me. I guess because they are me!

I moved around inside a layer of Earth called the mantle for a really, reeeeeeally long time. . . .

CRUST: The solid part of the planet you spend all your time on! It's super thin compared to the rest of Earth's layers, but as far as your daily lives go, the crust is your whole world.

MANTLE: This layer makes up most of the planet. It's immense! Even though the mantle seems solid to you humans, it does flow around if you watch it long enough—like I have!

OUTER CORE: Liquid, gooey, and hot hot hot! The outer core gets to be around 9,000 degrees Fahrenheit!

INNER CORE: The deepest layer. Temp-eratures here are even hotter than the outer core—maybe hotter than the surface of the sun! Holy geo-moly! You'd think it would be warm enough for everything to be melty, but the pressure of the planet pressing on the inner core keeps it totally solid.

3 BILLION YEARS AGO . . . Mantle time.

2 BILLION YEARS AGO . . . STILL mantle time. Wow, I was down there for ages.

Until . . .

No, not like pizza crust or a sandwich crust. You probably know Earth's crust better as the land and the ocean floor.

I got to know the ocean floor super well because the lava I was in cooled and became a part of it.

1.9 BILLION YEARS AGO . . .
Underwater volcano! My big debut!

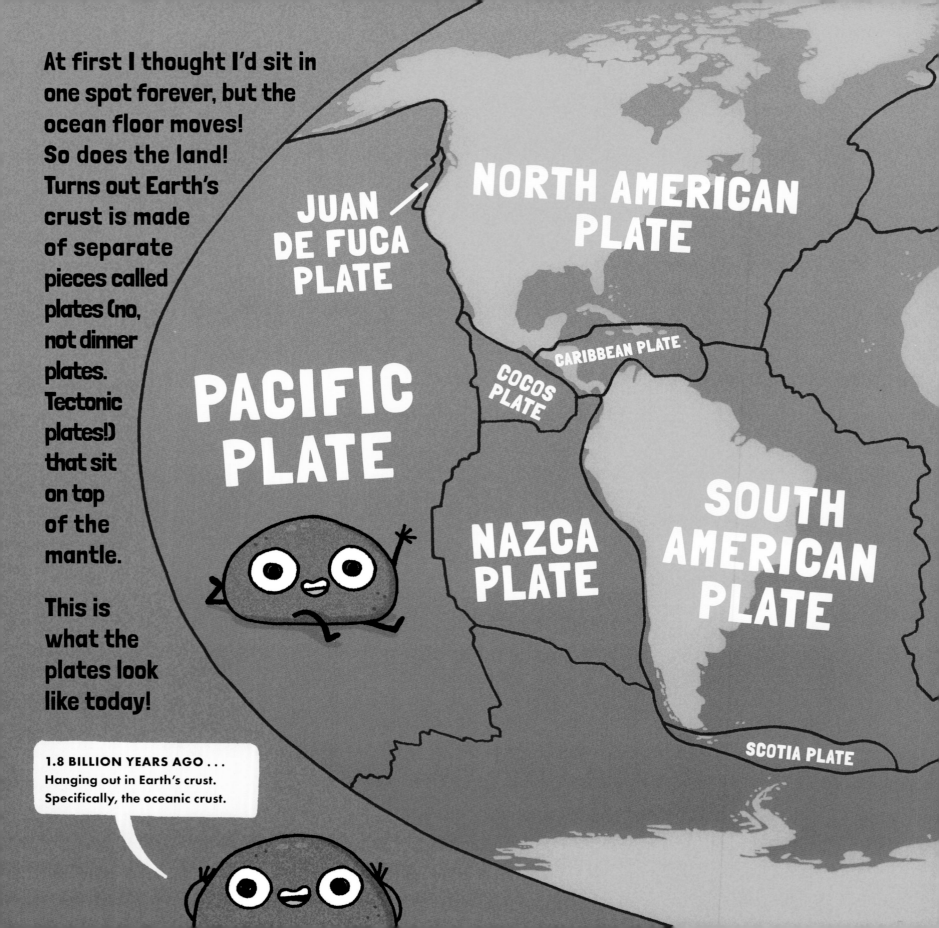

At first I thought I'd sit in one spot forever, but the ocean floor moves! So does the land! Turns out Earth's crust is made of separate pieces called plates (no, not dinner plates. Tectonic plates!) that sit on top of the mantle.

This is what the plates look like today!

1.8 BILLION YEARS AGO . . .
Hanging out in Earth's crust. Specifically, the oceanic crust.

JUAN DE FUCA PLATE

NORTH AMERICAN PLATE

CARIBBEAN PLATE

COCOS PLATE

PACIFIC PLATE

NAZCA PLATE

SOUTH AMERICAN PLATE

SCOTIA PLATE

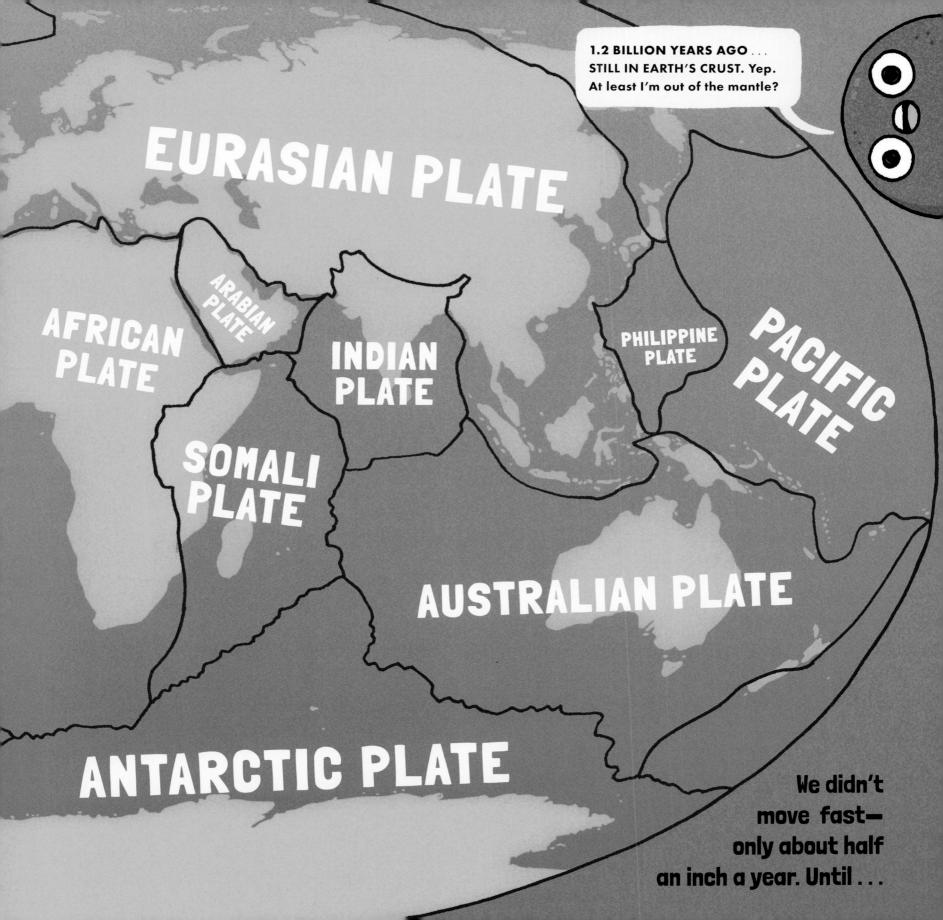

BOOM! SHAKE! BOOM!

**Our ocean plate sank under a land plate. I didn't know they could do that! We caused so many volcanoes and earthquakes on our way down.
Ah, whoops?**

I cooled and landed atop the actual land.

WOW.

WHAT A RIDE.

For the first time, I was me! Just me!

870 MILLION YEARS AGO . . .
Me, myself, and I. I for "igneous"!

An igneous rock, taking on the world! Until . . .

FUN FACT!

IGNEOUS: A rock that is made from liquid rock cooling into solid rock.

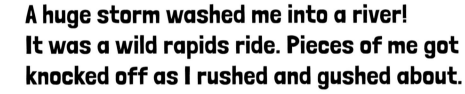

A huge storm washed me into a river! It was a wild rapids ride. Pieces of me got knocked off as I rushed and gushed about.

450 MILLION YEARS AGO . . .
A river ride I'll never forget!

445 MILLION YEARS AGO . . . Friends that became family. Our rock was called a conglomerate, and it was just the best. Ah, good times.

When the water settled, what was left of me was piled with other rocks. Over time, we ended up cemented together and became something new. Something sedimentary.

FUN FACT!

SEDIMENTARY: A rock that is made up of pieces of rocks, minerals, and sometimes even parts of animals or plants, all stuck together!

Then . . . **RUUUUUUUMBLE!**

Massive earthquake! I broke apart from the others and fell off a cliff into the ocean.

331 MILLION YEARS AGO . . . I'll never forget the day our conglomerate fell apart. Alas, tight groups crumble all the time, right? That's just how things go. It's okay; it's cool; it's fine! I'm fine. . . . I wonder what those rocks are up to these days.

SURF'S UP!

Did you know earthquakes can set off other natural disasters? I barely even had time to sink, because I ended up getting thrown back onto land by a huge wave—

it was a TSUNAMI!

325 MILLION YEARS AGO . . .
The famous supercontinent Pangaea formed, with me on it! I was there!

PHEW.

The continent I landed on squished into another and formed a supercontinent.
All the land in the world was connected then.

You can imagine the kinds of adventures I got into!

I was kicked by dinosaurs . . .

190 MILLION YEARS AGO . . .
Watch out for those theropods! Their feet are no joke.

FUN FACT!

SUPERCONTINENT: A huge continent that other continents eventually break off from. A new supercontinent forms about once every half a billion years, from smaller continents merging back together.

159 MILLION YEARS AGO . . .
I got to watch baby pterosaurs hatch. They were so adorable!

99 MILLION YEARS AGO . . .
There were some curious creatures back then that looked kind of like you all. Hmm . . .

lodged into a pterosaur nest . . .

sniffed by baby mammals . . .

buried in an avalanche . . .

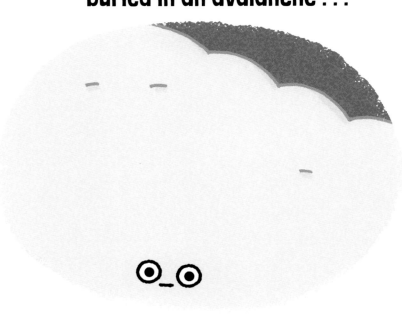

aaaand then . . .
stuck back in the ground.

As things piled **up, up, up . . .**

I got pushed

down,

down,

down.

95 MILLION YEARS AGO . . .
Buried again. Womp womp.

The weight of it all pushed on me so much, I *changed*. I became metamorphic. I still had all my minerals, but they were arranged in new ways. Shinier. Sparklier. I even had some pretty snazzy stripes for a while there.

But then I sank too far down and ended up melting back into magma.

84 MILLION YEARS AGO . . .
My metamorphosis was complete!

FUN FACT!

METAMORPHIC: Rock that gets its minerals rearranged (or even gets entirely new ones!) from increased heat, pressure, or other types of chemical change.

This time I didn't shoot out of a volcano.

Deep underground, there was no way of getting out.

Slowly, in the cold and dark,
I hardened into solid rock again.

It seemed my adventures were over.

I was trapped.

Or that's what I thought. What I didn't realize was that the plate I was in pushed against another. Together they bunched up to make a giant MOUNTAIN. But I was inside. I had no way to know!

HELLOOO? IT'S ME! I'M IN HERE!

70 MILLION YEARS AGO . . .
Rising up! Even though I didn't know it!

55 MILLION YEARS AGO . . . By this point, I was one of the highest things in the world. Wish I could've told myself that back then. I never would've believed it!

ROCK IS HERE!

Piece by piece, the rock around me crumbled away.

STILL RIGHT HERE . . .

EEE!

Then, one **AMAZING** day . . .

RIGHT ON THE EDGE!

UH-OH.

Daylight!
I eroded off the side of the mountain, free again! I tumbled down to the trees, back on land once more.

And that's where I've been
for the past few million years!

Well, until Luis stepped on me on the forest trail.

1 DAY AGO . . . I met Luis! Or at least, I met his shoe. And today I got to meet all of you!

So, there you have it! I might not look like much to all of you, but after four billion years, I'm proud to say that I'm here, I'm me, and . . .

Wow, you're here at the end of the book looking for even more to learn? That ROCKS!

You must be interested in **geology**—that's what you humans call the science of planet Earth. As cool as we are, there are *so* many things that geologists find fascinating besides us rocks. Geology is the study of how the entire planet works! Here, let me get you started with a list of . . .

AWESOME GEOLOGY FACTS!

• Earth is around 4.5 billion years old! It's one of eight planets in our solar system, which is one of billions of planetary systems in our galaxy, which is one of billions of galaxies in our universe. Imagine how many other planets must be out there!

• Earth's main layers are the crust, mantle, outer core, and inner core. To get to the inner core, you would need to drill down about 3,200 miles! No wonder humans have mostly explored only the crust.

• Earth's crust (the very top layer!) is made of pieces called **tectonic plates** that are always moving around. You don't notice the plates move because they usually go so slow (between the speed of your toenails growing and your hair growing), but when they move a little faster, that's when things get . . . *earthquake-y.*

• Earthquakes are measured by magnitude—a number that describes the strength of an earthquake. They can range from a tremor you humans can't even feel (magnitude 1.0) to catastrophic shaking that topples buildings and splits the ground open (up to magnitude 9.9)!

• Tectonic plate movements can also cause volcanoes. Volcanoes are a good reminder that under the solid surface, rock can be in a liquid form called **magma**. When enough pressure builds up, it can bubble out, trickle out, or even *explode* out as **lava**!

• When lava or magma cools into a solid rock, that type of rock is called **igneous**. The other main rock types are **sedimentary** (rock made of pieces of rock, silt, sand, mud, or bits of dead things) and **metamorphic** (rock changed by heat or pressure).

• The **rock cycle** is when rocks change types. The great thing about us rocks is that there's no order to our cycle! At any point, any of the main three types of rock can melt down, then refreeze and be igneous. Or crumble into sediment and form a sedimentary rock. Or get buried and have the pressure of the planet turn us metamorphic. We go with the flow, you know?

• Rocks are made of minerals. Geologists like to call **minerals** "rock ingredients." Most rocks (like me!) are made out of many different minerals, but some, like quartz or chalk, are made of just one.

• Gemstones are rocks that you humans seem to like a whole bunch. And who can blame you? They are usually made of just one mineral, and often in a beautiful crystal form, like a diamond, ruby, or peridot.

• You can learn about Earth's history from minerals in ancient rocks or from special rocks called **fossils**! Fossils are formed when minerals seep into and harden up things that prehistoric life left behind, like bones, footprints, and even poop!

• It's not just rocks that teach about Earth's past. Ice can too! Air bubbles can be trapped in ice. You can learn what the atmosphere was like millions of years ago by drilling into ice and pulling out long cylinders called **ice cores**. The deeper you go, the older the trapped air bubbles!

• Speaking of ice, did you know ice moves? Glaciers are like frozen rivers of ice. They flow like slow-motion water! They can be miles high and dramatically change the landscape they move over!

Liquid water can also change the shape of the land! For [exa]mple, canyons are places where water has worn down, [e]roded, the ground to make deep crevasses. (Sometimes [it] can reveal rocks as old as *me*!) You can try this yourself [by p]ouring a bucket of water on a beach or a sandbox and [wat]ching it carve through the sand.

Even *air* can shape the planet. Wind can erode a mountain, [giv]en enough time! And sometimes air can move rocks around the globe. Sand from Africa has been found all the way over in the Americas, carried on winds across the ocean!

- Final fun fact: lightning can change rocks. Yes, *lightning*. When lightning strikes, it heats up the ground. This can cause the sand, rocks, and minerals below to fuse together into a structure called **fulgurite**. Fulgurite looks like a lightning bolt frozen in time!

Cool stuff, huh? Humans often think of us rocks as steady and unchanging, but in my experience, we can change a whole lot. Just like you, I bet! Now for a . . .

GEOLOGY POP QUIZ!

[W]hat kind of rock was I at the end of the book?

A. Sedimentary

B. Metamorphic

C. Igneous

D. All the above!

Answer: C! I was each different type of rock at diff[erent] points in my story, but after melting into magma and co[oling] again near the end, I became igneous once m[ore.]

[W]hat layer of Earth can humans touch?

A. Mantle

B. Crust

C. Core

D. All the above!

Answer: B! Maybe one day you all will reach the other [sec]tions, but so far, humans have never been to the mantle, [outer] core, or inner core. Only us rocks have been down t[here.]

[W]hat can happen when two tectonic plates move [quic]kly against each other?

A. Earthquake

B. Volcano

C. Tsunami

D. All the above!

Answer: D! Tectonic plates can make things get [...]

Now that you've heard my geology tale, it's time to get out there and explore Earth yourself! Remember, every rock you pick up has a story to share.

SOURCES

Lea, Robert. "How Big Is Earth?" Space.com, July 6, 2021. https://www.space.com/17638-how-big-is-earth.html.

Marshak, Stephen. *Earth: Portrait of a Planet,* 1st ed. New York, NY: W. W. Norton and Company, 2001.

NASA. "Welcome to the Universe." NASA.gov, 2024. https://science.nasa.gov/universe.

National Geographic Society. "Plate Tectonics," National Geographic Education, March 7, 2024. https://education .nationalgeographic.org/resource/plate-tectonics.

"What Are Minerals?" Geology.com. 2024. https://geology.com/minerals.

United States Geological Society. "Geology," 2024. https://www.usgs.gov/science/faqs/geology